Wide Range Readers
Readers

BLUE BOOK 5

Fred J. Schonell

Phyllis Flowerdew

Oliver & Boyd

Illustrated by Alexa Rutherford
Cover illustration by Gordon Melville

OLIVER & BOYD
Croythorn House
23 Ravelston Terrace
Edinburgh EH4 3TJ
A division of Longman Group Ltd.

First published 1949
Second Edition 1965
Third Edition 1976
Reprinted 1977

ISBN 0 05 002915 0

Set in 12/18pt 'Monophoto' Plantin
Printed in Hong Kong by
Sheck Wah Tong Printing Press

Preface

These books have been planned to meet the particular needs of children whose reading ages fall between seven years and eleven years plus.[1] The books are graded by control of vocabulary and sentence structure. Books 1 to 4 are graded in half years, and Books 5 and 6 by single years, thus providing for individual variations in reading ability within any section or group.

There are two series, Blue Books and Green Books. They are parallel and of comparable difficulty. Some children will need to complete one colour only. It does not matter which. Others will read, for example, Blue Book 1, and will need further practice at the same level (i.e. Green Book 1), before going on to Blue Book 2.

The story element is predominant, with adequate repetition in the early books. Some informative material is included to stimulate and foster the development of interests and intellectual curiosity. Further material of this kind is provided by The Wide Range Interest Books and The New Interest Books.

Illustrations and care in printing, particularly in the spacing between words and lines and in the placing of reading units have been employed with maximum effect to facilitate quick recognition of words and phrases and adequate understanding of sentences.

This carefully planned approach and gradual increase of difficulty should ensure success for all children and should lead them on confidently to wider reading.

[1] Pupils with reading ages below 7 years should continue with a book suited to their reading age, e.g. in the *Happy Venture Readers*. Reading age may be found from the Graded Word Reading Test in *The Psychology and Teaching of Reading*, F.J. Schonell and E. Goodacre (Oliver & Boyd), Fifth Revised Edition.

Contents

The Ski Race

Down the snow-covered mountain side went Franz on skis. So swiftly he went, that from the distance he looked almost like a bird flying past. The wind met him in a little rush, and his skis sent tiny fountains of powdered snow into the air.

Franz was ten years old, and he had learnt to ski almost as soon as he had learnt to walk, for his home had always been high up in the mountains of Austria.

He rested a moment, and looked down below at the dark green fir trees laden with snow. Beyond the trees he could see the village with its wooden houses nestling in the valley, and the morning sun glinting on the windows of the painted church. Summer in

Austria was lovely, but winter was almost too beautiful to be true.

On the westward slopes people were moving about —small and far away—putting red flags in the snow. They were getting the course ready for the ski races. Franz smiled. This was the most important day of his life. This afternoon at three o'clock the ski races were to begin. His name was down on the list for children under twelve. Oh, if only he could win! The village children were very fast. They had played and practised together every week-end for months. Franz usually had to practise alone, for his sister was only a baby, and his house was far from the village. But he was fast too, and he knew that if everything went well, he ought to win. He did want to win. He wanted to win the ski race more than anything else in the world!

But no. There was one thing he wanted even more than that. He wanted to meet Karl Engels. Karl Engels was the champion skier of Austria, and the holder of the speed record for Europe. How wonderful it would be to see him—to speak to him! Franz sighed.

"I'll practise once more," he said to himself, "and then I'll go indoors and rest."

He pretended that this was the actual race, and that

the baby fir tree just ahead was the winning post. Away he went. The wind met him in a little rush, and his skis left a smooth narrow track in the snow behind him. He pretended that Karl Engels waited at the winning post. And when Franz passed the baby fir tree, and won the pretend race, Karl came forward and shook hands and said,

"That was a fine bit of skiing, Franz!" If only such a thing would really happen!

*　　*　　*

At dinner time Franz's mother said,

"You'll go directly after dinner, won't you, Franz. Then you will have time to rest before the race starts."

"Yes, Mother." His eyes shone with excitement, for it was nearly time for the race at last.

"I'm sorry I can't come to watch you," went on Mother, "but Father is too ill to be left alone."

"Yes. I'm sorry too."

"Never mind. You'll be able to tell me all about it when you come back."

"Do you think I shall win, Mother?"

"I shouldn't be at all surprised. You've worked hard, and you are fast for your age. Why, one day you might become the champion skier of Austria, and the holder of the speed record for Europe!"

"Oh, yes!"

These pleasant thoughts were interrupted by a voice from upstairs.

"Father is calling," said Franz. "Shall I go to him?"

"No. You finish your dinner." Mother went out of the room, and Franz heard the sound of her footsteps on the wooden stairs. Poor Father! He had been ill so long. He must be tired of lying in bed all day when the sun was shining and the snow was gleaming. How he must long to be up, and doing his work again.

In the summer Franz's father was a mountain guide, and in the winter he gave skiing lessons on the slopes above the village.

He had other work too. He had to look after the hut near the mountain top, because his house was nearest to it.

The hut was stout and strong, and its door was always left unlocked, so that anyone wandering up there in the heights could walk in at any time and shelter for the night. There was a way across the mountains from the east, and in the summer climbers came with rucksacks and ropes and ice axes, and the hut was often used. Travellers always found bunks and blankets for sleeping, a lamp for light, and pots and pans, a can of oil, and a stove for cooking. Franz's father went up from time to time to see that everything was all right, and to take more oil to put into the can.

In winter he did not go so often, for the hut had fewer visitors. But even so, there were men making ski tours across the mountains, sleeping in different huts each night, trying out their strength, and watching the white beauty of winter in the peaks.

Suddenly Mother came into the room again. She looked worried.

"Oh, Franz," she said. "Someone will have to take oil up to the hut."

Franz sat quite still. Fancy forgetting the hut!

9.

Father had not been there for weeks and weeks. The oil must be getting low. Surely the can must be empty by now. Skiers would arrive, cold and tired and hungry. They would not be able to light the lamp, or use the stove to cook their food. *Someone* would have to take oil up for them.

"Tomorrow," thought Franz. But tomorrow might be too late. People might arrive at the hut tonight, and find no oil.

"It's the ski race today," said Franz in a whisper.

"I know," murmured Mother, and she looked so unhappy that Franz turned his eyes away.

"I can't leave Father," said Mother softly. From upstairs came the sound of Father coughing. The baby awoke from sleep, and began to cry.

"I'll go to the hut, Mother," said Franz. "I know the way. I went twice last summer with Father."

"It is harder in the winter, and there is no time to get there and back today."

"I can stay the night in the hut, and return home early in the morning."

"You'll miss the ski race," murmured Mother.

"It doesn't matter," said Franz. "It doesn't matter a bit."

But of course it did matter, and Franz felt very sad as he packed his rucksack with food for supper and breakfast, fastened the can of oil to his back, and fixed his skis to his feet.

"Goodbye," he said.

His mother, holding the baby, watched him go. He was a good skier. She was not worried about that. He was a good climber too, and the way up from this side was really quite easy. But he would miss the ski race —and he looked small to be going up there in the clouds alone.

Franz followed a little path through a patch of fir trees, where the snow was crisp and hard like ice, and his progress was slow because he had to dig his skis in sideways on the slope. Then, when he had passed the trees, he travelled across the mountain and back again in wide zig-zag tracks, each one above the one before it. A sound came to his ears—the sound of distant shouting and cheering. The ski races had started. He had practised so hard. He had looked forward to the ski race for so long, and now he was missing it. This was to have been the most important day of his life, and now it was spoiled.

That afternoon, just as the sun went down, Franz

reached the hut. All alone in the heights it stood—
brown and weather-beaten, with a thick blanket of
snow on the roof, and piles of snow against its wooden
sides.

Franz was very tired. He wondered if anyone *would*
go to the hut that night. Perhaps it would be empty,
and he might have gone to the ski race after all. He
might have won it, and been back at home telling
Mother all about it by now.

He pushed open the hut door, and as he went in,
he heard voices. He heard a man say,

"Oh, well, if there's no oil, we can't even make ourselves a cup of coffee. Bad luck, isn't it?"

There were two men there—one fair and the other dark. In the half darkness of the hut, they saw Franz standing shyly by the door.

"Hullo!" said one. "You've come to a very poor hut. There's not a drop of oil in the place. Not a drop!"

"Good gracious!" exclaimed the other. "It's only a boy! Whatever are you doing up here all alone?"

"I've brought the oil," said Franz.

In a very short time the lamp and the stove were alight, the hut was warm and cosy, and Franz and the two men were eating a fine supper, and sipping hot coffee. The men were so friendly and kind, and so grateful to Franz for bringing the oil, that soon he found himself telling them all that had happened. He told them about Father being ill, and not able to come to the hut. He told them about himself, and how he wanted to be a champion skier when he grew older—champion of Austria, holder of the speed record for Europe, like Karl Engels. He told them about the ski race he had hoped to win.

"And now I've missed it," he ended sadly.

"Well, I think you're a very brave boy," said one,

"and I'm proud to meet you."

"And you haven't told us your name yet," said the other. "What is it?"

"Franz."

"Mine is Julius," said the man with fair hair.

"And mine is Karl," added the dark one, leaning forward to shake hands. Franz's eyes opened wide as the lamp light shone on his new friend's face. He had seen that face before! Of course he had. He'd seen photographs of it in every paper. It was the face of the champion skier of Austria, the holder of the speed record for Europe.

"Karl?" murmured Franz in wonder.

"Karl Engels," said Karl with a smile.

★　　★　　★

So Franz slept the night in the hut with Karl and Julius. Early next day they arose and had breakfast, leaving everything tidy and clean, ready for the next travellers who should pass that way. Then they closed the door, and fastened on their skis. The air was cold, for though it was nearly light, the sun had not yet risen above the mountains.

"I have to go this way," said Franz, pointing across the snow.

"We'll come with you part of the way," replied Julius. "Then when your house comes into sight, we'll branch off to the west."

"Can you spare the time?" asked Franz.

"Oh, yes," said Karl. "Besides, we want to see what your skiing is like."

Down the slope they started—Karl first, then Franz, then Julius, each keeping the same distance from the others—following Karl's tracks in a wide zig-zag pattern down the mountain side. The wind met them in a cold little rush, and their skis sent tiny fountains of powdered snow into the air.

After a while Karl stood and waited for the others to catch up with him. He watched Franz coming nearer. Down the slope came Franz. His eyes shone and his heart was full of happiness. His skis seemed to skim over the ground without effort. He seemed almost to fly. But what would Karl think of his skiing? Would he—would he think it was good?

As Franz reached the end of the slope, Karl Engels came forward with a smile of admiration on his sun-burnt face.

"That was a fine bit of skiing, Franz," he said.

And at that moment the sun rose above the mountain. The snow sparkled against a sky suddenly blue, and the mountain peaks glowed pink and gold, as one by one they were bathed in the glory of morning.

The Man who Minded the House

Once upon a time a farmer was working in the fields, where the hay was lying spread out to dry in the sun. It was a beautiful evening, but the farmer was tired and cross.

"My work never ends," he thought. "Tomorrow I shall have to gather up all this hay, and store it in the barn—and I'm so tired." Wearily he put the hay fork away, and went into his cottage.

His wife was sitting in a rocking chair by the window, rocking gently to and fro, and humming a tune to herself. She had put the baby to bed, and cooked the supper and set the table. She had only just that minute sat down, and there was her husband home already. She looked up and smiled at him, but he didn't smile back at her. He only frowned and said crossly,

"I wish I had nothing to do all day but to rock to and fro in the rocking chair—like you."

"Oh, but I've only just sat down," said his wife. "I've been busy since early morning."

"Doing what?" asked the farmer.

"Well," said his wife, "there's Baby to look after, and I've polished the floors and dusted the rooms, and

17

done the dishes, and made the beds. I've cooked the food, and seen to the cow, and washed some clothes."

"Those are easy things," said the farmer. "I wouldn't mind doing easy jobs like that."

"Easy things!" exclaimed his wife. "I'd like to see *you* do my day's work."

"All right," said the farmer angrily, "tomorrow we'll change over. I'll do the housework and look after the baby, while you go and gather up the hay from the fields."

"All right," agreed his wife, "we will."

She went into the kitchen to fetch the supper, and as she served it out, she said to herself,

"Easy jobs! He'll soon see!"

Next morning after breakfast the farmer was very cheerful.

"I shall have a nice, peaceful day," he said. "As soon as you have gone, I shall get all the work done, and then I shall sit in the rocking chair, and rock to and fro for the rest of the day."

"Remember to bring Baby downstairs and give her some breakfast in about half an hour, won't you?" said his wife, putting on her sun hat to shade her eyes.

"Yes, I'll remember."

"And this is the day the butter must be churned."

"That won't take me long."

"And don't forget to take the cow across to the meadow, will you?"

"No, I won't forget."

"And you'll call me when the dinner's ready, won't you?"

"Yes, yes, I'll call you."

The wife started walking towards the barn, to fetch the hay fork. Then she stopped, and shouted,

"Are you quite sure you still want to change over work for the day?"

"Quite sure," he answered. "I'm going to enjoy myself."

So the wife went away to the fields to gather up the hay, put it in the cart, and store it up in the barn. The farmer waved goodbye, and then turned back into the house.

"I'll churn the butter first," he thought. "That won't take me long." He poured the cream into the churn, and turned the handle. After a few moments, he looked inside to see if the cream had turned into butter. But oh, no, it was not nearly thick enough, so he turned the handle again. He turned it and turned it and turned it, until he felt quite hot and tired. And still the cream was not thick enough.

"I'll get a drink before I do any more," thought the farmer. He went down to the cellar where there was a barrel of his wife's home-made ginger beer, with a small tap fixed in the side. He turned on the tap, and held a glass beneath it.

Suddenly he heard a strange noise.

"Ook, ook, ook!"

"What can that be?" he wondered. "Oh, I know! The pig must be loose." Quickly he put down the glass and hurried up the stairs, forgetting that the ginger beer was still running out of the tap. But oh, dear, just as he reached the kitchen there was a crash! The pig had walked in through the open kitchen door, and had knocked over the butter churn.

"Oh!" said the farmer to the pig, "however did you get out of your sty?" He tried to drive the pig back through the door, but the pig became frightened, and ran in and out among the furniture. Meanwhile the cream from the churn was running all over the kitchen floor. And down below in the cellar, the ginger beer had filled the glass to overflowing and was splashing out all over the floor as well.

The farmer made a sudden rush at the pig. The pig darted out of the door, but the farmer slipped, and fell on his back in a pool of thick, cold, sticky cream.

As he stood slowly up on his feet again, he remembered the ginger beer. Down to the cellar he rushed, but he was too late. The barrel was empty, and the ginger beer was lying in a flood all over the cellar floor.

"Whatever will my wife say?" he thought, and he stood there for a moment, wondering how to clear up the mess. Then he heard, "Moo, moo, moo," and he suddenly remembered the cow.

"Poor thing," he said to himself. "It's getting late, and the cow is still in the shed. I'd better take her to the meadow before I do anything else."

Now the farmhouse was built close up against a steep hill, so that if you came down the hillside, you could jump on to the roof. In fact, there was a crop of grass growing on the roof top, so that it was hardly possible to tell which was roof and which was hillside.

As the farmer walked along to the cowshed, he had an idea. Why bother to take the cow all the way to the meadow? She could eat the grass from the roof instead. He managed to get the cow on to the grassy roof. Then he went into the kitchen to clean up the mess.

To his surprise he saw that it was nearly dinner time.

"Whatever am I going to cook for dinner?" he asked himself. "And I haven't washed up the breakfast things yet."

He filled a kettle with water, and put it on the stove. He quickly peeled some potatoes, and put them in a pot to boil. At that moment the baby started crying.

"Good gracious! I haven't even fed the baby yet!" murmured the farmer. Just as he was going upstairs to fetch her, he thought of the cow again.

"She might fall off the roof and hurt herself," he

said aloud. "I'd better make sure that she's safe."

So he went on to the roof, and tied a piece of rope round the cow's neck. He slipped the other end of the rope down the chimney, so that it dangled below in the kitchen. Then he went indoors again, and tied the rope round his own waist.

"Now for the baby's food," said he.

At the same time he began thinking how nice it must be out in the field tossing hay. His wife's work wasn't easy after all. He had lots to do before he could call her in to dinner. He had two floors to clean, the baby to feed, dishes to wash, beds to make, and dinner to prepare. Perhaps his wife wouldn't notice how late it was getting. He wondered if he could ask her to let him do his own work in the afternoon. A whole day was such a long time in which to be doing difficult jobs like these.

"Wow, wow, wow!" cried the baby. No doubt she wondered why no one came to fetch her or to feed her.

Now the cow was munching grass on the roof, and moving nearer and nearer to the edge, and the wife was out in the fields, thinking, "It *must* be dinner time. Why doesn't my husband call me?"

She laughed as she tossed the hay into the cart. "I

guess he's had enough of housework," she thought. She waited a little longer, and then decided to go home without waiting to be called. She left the hay fork standing against the cart, and started to walk along the path towards home.

Just then, the cow fell off the roof, and the rope dragged the farmer up the chimney. As the wife drew near to the house, she saw the cow dangling about in the air. She ran forward and cut the rope. Down came the cow outside, and down came the farmer inside.

Then she opened the kitchen door, and said with a smile, "Well, how did you like doing my work? Was it easy?"

Her husband crawled out from the fireplace where he had fallen. He was black with soot, and where he wasn't black with soot, he was white with cream. He was so miserable that he could not even answer. He just looked sadly at his wife, and she knew exactly what he thought about her work now.

And that is the end of the story, except of course that the farmer never, never again suggested that he should stay at home and do the housework.

Adapted

24

The Hayloft

Through all the pleasant meadow-side
The grass grew shoulder-high,
Till the shining scythes went far and wide
And cut it down to dry.

Those green and sweetly smelling crops
They led in waggons home;
And they piled them here in mountain tops
For mountaineers to roam.

Here is Mount Clear, Mount Rusty-Nail,
Mount Eagle and Mount High;
The mice that in these mountains dwell,
No happier are than I!

O, what a joy to clamber there,
O, what a place for play,
With the sweet, the dim, the dusty air,
The happy hills of hay!

ROBERT LOUIS STEVENSON

Eros

Piccadilly Circus is the name of a place in the centre of London where many streets meet. In the middle of Piccadilly there is a small island of stone, and on this island there is a statue called Eros. Eros holds a bow and arrow, and leans forward as if he is flying over London. On the steps below him women used to sit with baskets of violets and snowdrops, or bunches of pink carnations and tight little rosebuds.

All around are buses and lorries, and taxis and cars coming from north and south and east and west. Day after day the busy London traffic swirls round the small, stone island, and day after day people hurry past on their way to shops and theatres and stations and offices.

Everyone knows Eros. Taxi drivers look up at him, and say,

"Ah, Eros! Here we are at Piccadilly!"

Children, holding tightly to their mothers' hands as they cross the road, try to catch a glimpse of him between the rows of traffic. But no one seems to have time to go up the steps, and read the words that are written below the statue. And many people, though they know Eros so well, do not know at all why he is there.

He is there to remind them of a story about a man called the Earl of Shaftesbury, who spent his whole life helping children.

In those days it was no fun to be a child. Most children, unless they were rich, had no time to play, and very little time even to sleep.

They worked in factories and mills from early in the morning till late at night. They worked on farms and brick fields. They climbed up chimneys to sweep away soot. They crawled down mines to push along trucks of coal. These children did not know what it was like to be clean and happy.

The Earl of Shaftesbury was rich, yet when he was a child, he was unhappy too. His father was always busy, and his mother was interested only in going to parties and wearing beautiful clothes. Even the servants sometimes forgot about him. So the little boy was often lonely in his big house, and sad because it seemed as if no one cared for him.

Perhaps that was why, when he grew up, he cared so much, and worked so hard for unhappy children.

At first he wondered what he could do to help them.

He had not enough money to feed all the hungry ones, or to take all the ill ones away from the work that tired them, but there was something he could do. He could go into Parliament, and try to make Parliament pass laws to help the children of England.

He started with the children in factories and mills, where wool, silk and cotton cloth were made. He visited one factory after another, watching and talking to poor little girls and boys of six and seven, and even four and five years of age, who worked the machines. They had to get up at three in the morning, while it was dark, and they were still half asleep, and they had to work till ten o'clock at night. The Earl of Shaftesbury noticed how thin and pale they were, and he knew that though they were hungry, they were usually too tired even to eat.

For a long while he worked hard, writing and making speeches, and at last Parliament listened to him, and passed a law saying that no children were to work in factories.

Then he looked round for other unhappy children, and he decided to help those who worked in coal mines. The underground passages in mines were very narrow, so the tiniest children were sent to crawl along them, pulling the trucks of coal. These children hardly ever saw sunshine and blue skies. They were always in the dark, with not even enough space for growing properly, but soon the Earl of Shaftesbury's work set them free too.

Now there were chimney sweep boys who needed his help. Chimneys were wide in those days, and small boys were made to climb up inside them, to clean them. Many were the nights in which the Earl of Shaftesbury lay awake thinking about them. He wrote letters to the papers, and made speeches in Parliament, until a law was made to save these children too.

After that, he helped children who worked on farms and brick fields, and he built schools and homes for them.

In London he found hundreds of children who just wandered about the streets, because they had no one to look after them. They had no homes to shelter them, so at night they slept in doorways and under arches. He had a big ship sent to the River Thames, and there the homeless children were able to live, with good food to eat, clean beds to sleep in, and kind people to look after them.

There was no end to the kindness of the Earl of

Shaftesbury. Year by year he worked, until, by the time he was an old man, there were hardly any unhappy children left in England.

When he died, money was collected for a statue by which to remember him. The people who gave the money in shillings and sixpences and pennies were the children whom he had helped. They were grown up by then, but they remembered how this great man had saved them from heavy work as young children in factories and on farms, in mines and mills, and brick fields and chimneys, and they remembered how he had given them freedom and happiness.

And the statue that was set up in his memory was the statue of Eros on the small stone island in Piccadilly Circus in the centre of London.

Grandfather's Ship

People wondered why Don had chosen to become a deep sea diver. There were so many other things he could have been. Whatever had put such an idea into his mind?

"Who suggested it?" he was asked.

"No one," Don always replied. But though no one had actually mentioned deep sea diving to him, it was a story that his grandfather had told him long ago that had first given him the idea.

Don had been a little boy then, staying in Grandfather's white cottage that stood high on the cliffs, overlooking the sea. It happened like this.

Grandfather sat in the window seat, puffing at his pipe, and watching the distant curls of foam on the sea.

"It must be nice to watch the sea every day," said Don, sitting down beside him.

"I've watched the sea every day of my life," replied Grandfather, slowly.

"Even when you were a boy?" asked Don, hoping he might get the old man to tell him a story.

"Yes. As long as I can remember I've slept in the

room above, with my bed close to the window facing the sea."

"Ships don't often pass this way, do they?"

"No. It's a lonely bit of coast."

Grandfather's eyes gleamed suddenly at a memory, and he leaned forward and said in a hushed voice,

"Once I saw—"

Then he stopped.

"What did you see?" asked Don.

"Oh, nothing," murmured Grandfather.

"Tell me," urged Don.

"What is the good?" said Grandfather. "I've told dozens of people, and no one has ever believed me."

"Please tell me."

Don looked so anxious and excited that Grandfather could not say no to him. So the story was told, and all the time streaks of white foam curled backwards and forwards on the distant sea.

"One night long ago," said Grandfather, "there was a terrible storm. The wind rattled the doors as if it would shake the cottage to pieces, and even from this distance I could hear the angry roar of the sea. I was very small, and hadn't even learnt to speak properly. I sat up in bed and looked out into the darkness. At the other side of the room my brother went on sleeping. I remember hearing a loud crack, as the wind tore a branch from the apple tree in the garden, and then—then—"

"Yes?" whispered Don.

"There was a flash of lightning. It seemed to split the sky in two. And in that moment of light I saw a ship go down. So great and beautiful she was, with her masts pointing to the sky, and all her sails setting like folded shadows. So beautiful—and she was gone."

"Oh!" murmured Don, and it seemed to him that he could hear the storm, and see the ship sinking.

34

"In the morning," continued Grandfather, "my mother was sad to see the apple tree broken, and my father had to mend the gate, which the wind had damaged. I tried to tell them about the ship, but they did not understand. They only said, 'Go and play, Martin,' and went on talking about the gate and the apple tree."

"And didn't they ever understand?" asked Don.

"Yes. Years later when I could speak plainly, I told them again. They said I had dreamt it. They said that if a ship had really gone down, someone else would have seen it too, or at least heard of it. My brother teased me about dreaming, and after that, if anything sounded impossible, the family always laughed and said, 'Like Martin's ship.' They have said that all through the years. People still say it, only now they say 'Grandfather's ship' instead."

Grandfather moved in his chair, and sighed.

"No one believes me," he added.

"I do!" exclaimed Don. "I believe you."

He stared out at the sea for a long while, his eyes shining, and his mind full of the story.

"Such a beautiful ship she was," said Grandfather again, "such a beautiful ship."

And then the idea had come to Don, that when he grew up, he would become a deep sea diver, and one day he would dive into that same stretch of sea, and find Grandfather's ship for him.

So here he was, grown up, and trained as a deep sea diver, and here he was in a rowing boat with his friend Derek, in the very stretch of sea where Grandfather's ship had gone down.

"This is the place," said Don, bringing the boat to a standstill.

"Lovely calm day," murmured Derek. "I say," he added. "Don't be disappointed if you don't find anything, will you? I mean, your grandfather *might* have dreamt it or imagined it."

"Yes, he might," replied Don, "but he still believes that he saw the ship, and somehow I've always believed it too." He pulled on three pairs of thick socks, and put three woollen jerseys on over his clothes. It was hot up here in the sun, but he knew it would be cold at the bottom of the sea. He fastened pads on his shoulders, and then put on his rubber diving suit, and boots with lead soles.

"Good luck!" said Derek, and he slipped the helmet over Don's head, and screwed it firmly in place. Don climbed on to the ladder leading from the boat down into the water. He waited while Derek arranged the air pipe by which he was to breathe, and the lead weights which were to help him to sink to the bottom. Derek started the air pump. Don waved his hand, climbed down the ladder, and slid down the rope hanging beneath.

In a few seconds he was standing at the bottom of the sea. At first he saw nothing but sand beneath his feet, misty grey sea water all around, and a few startled fish swimming away. Then he saw twisting strands of seaweed, and strange sea creatures of red and pink. But he could not see a ship. He walked about on the floor of the ocean, looking through the glass window of his helmet, searching everywhere.

Perhaps Grandfather's ship had been a dream after all, or perhaps already the sand had buried it for ever. On and on went Don, but it was no good. Wherever he went, there were only coloured fish and straggling seaweeds.

Sadly he walked back, and pulled at the life line, to show Derek that he was coming up again. Don knew that it was dangerous for a diver to stay down too long, and also that it was dangerous to rise to the surface too quickly. As he went higher and higher he rested several times on the rope. Then at last he came to the ladder, and Derek helped him carefully into the boat.

As soon as Don's helmet was off, Derek asked, "Did you find the ship?"

Wearily Don shook his head. When he had rested a while, and become used to breathing fresh air again, he said,

"Let's row further out, and try again."

"All right," agreed Derek, taking the oars.

So once more, in even deeper water, Don went down to the bottom of the sea. As before, he saw nothing at first except sand and misty grey sea water. Then he saw gaily-coloured sea creatures and strands of curly seaweed—and rocks a little way ahead.

"I guess Grandfather did dream it after all," he thought. He walked round the rocks, moving carefully so that his air pipe should not get tangled. And there before him was a great shadow. Could it be? He hardly dared to hope. He remembered Grandfather saying,

"So beautiful she was, with her masts pointing to the sky, and all her sails setting like folded shadows."

Oh, if Grandfather could only see what Don was seeing now!

There stood the ship half buried in the sand, with shell fish and seaweeds clinging to her sides, and black and scarlet fish swimming across her decks. The masts and the sails had been broken and washed away. There were gaping cracks and broken doors where cabins had once been, and huge holes where the wood was rotting. Slowly the ship was breaking up, there at the bottom of the sea—but oh, she was beautiful still!

"I must take something for Grandfather," thought Don, "even if it's only a bit of wood."

He looked round, and climbed in and out among the wreckage. She was a foreign ship, he could tell, and he wondered from which country she had sailed so bravely in the days when Grandfather had been a little boy.

There was one cabin Don could not enter, for the door still hung firmly in place, and was wedged so tightly that it would not open. He leaned his shoulder against it, and pushed with all his strength.

The door burst open suddenly, and Don stumbled inside, almost falling against a small iron box in the corner.

"What's this?" he said to himself, stooping to lift the box. At that moment he felt a tug at his life line. That was Derek saying,

"Time to come up."

Oh, he must just peep in this old box first! Quickly he pulled open the rusty lid—and there inside were coins—golden coins! Another tug came at the life line.

"You've been under long enough. You must come up at once," Derek was trying to say.

But here were golden coins, hundreds and hundreds of them—treasure from a foreign land!

"This is something to take to Grandfather!" said Don aloud, and clinging to the box, he climbed out of the cabin, and started going up and up through the misty grey water, leaving the ship alone and beautiful, like a shadow on the floor of the sea.

Did You Know This?

If you approach a lapwing's nest, the bird will sometimes hop away, pretending to have a broken wing. It does this so that you will look at it or follow it, instead of walking on and perhaps finding its eggs or its young ones.

The gold-crested wren, which is one of the smallest British birds, weighs only 28 grams. But this wren is a determined little chap, and every year he crosses the North Sea during migration. No doubt he knows when the right wind is blowing, and is able to decide upon the best time to make the long sea crossing.

Other birds of course travel thousands of kilometres during their flights from cold countries to warmer lands for the winter.

Some birds lay eggs that are almost the exact

colouring of their surroundings. So even when you are almost on top of the eggs, you find it difficult to see them, because they are so much like the earth or the stones or the bushes.

When salmon are swimming, they sometimes jump waterfalls, in order to continue their journey upstream.

The lobster is rather clever. If an enemy seizes hold of one of its legs, the lobster casts off the leg that is caught. It does not seem to come to any harm by doing this, and it is able to hurry away to a place of safety.

Have you ever wondered how pearls are made? A little piece of sand or grit finds its way into an oyster shell. The oyster is irritated by this, and he sends out a fluid called nacre, which flows over the sand or grit, and covers it. In this way a pearl is formed.

When Anna Danced

The theatre was full. In a few moments the chattering would stop, and the lights would be dimmed. In a few moments the curtains would part, and the ballet would begin.

Anna dangled her thin legs, and looked round in wonder at all the people—so many people. Some of them wore beautiful clothes and shining jewels. Anna's mother had no beautiful clothes or shining jewels, for she was poor, and had to work hard to buy even enough food to eat. Anna moved a little closer to her.

"When I grow up," she thought, "I'll earn a lot of money, so that I can buy pretty frocks and warm fur coats for Mother." She wondered what she would be when she grew older. Perhaps she would be an artist, for she liked drawing. Then she could buy a big house, and Mother would not have to work any more. Their own house was so small, and Mother was always worrying about things they needed but could not afford to buy, and about clothes that wore out too quickly.

At that moment the curtains moved just the tiniest bit, and all the long velvet folds shivered as if a breeze were passing by. Quickly Anna looked in front of her.

She didn't want to miss anything. But the curtain was still again, and nothing happened after all.

"I wonder if it's still snowing outside," whispered Anna. Mother smiled.

"It's nice and warm in here," she said.

"When will the curtains open, Mother?"

"Very soon, now."

"What is the ballet called, Mother?"

"The Sleeping Beauty."

The Sleeping Beauty. That was a story Anna had always loved. How interesting it would be to see it acted and danced upon a stage.

Anna was eight years old, and this was the first time

she had ever been to a theatre. Mother had saved and saved to buy the tickets. It was a special treat.

There was music. The curtains shivered again. Slowly they parted. Slowly they opened. Anna's eyes opened too—wide and wondering, for she saw a room in a King's palace, and a baby princess lying in a golden cradle. Watching over the baby were nurses in pink, and nurses in blue, who pulled a golden cord to rock the cradle to and fro. Down the steps and into the room came the King and Queen, and all the people who had come to see the baby. There were noblemen in velvet suits of black and crimson. There were ladies in silk and satin.

Then came the fairies, each with a present and a wish for the little princess. The Lilac Fairy came, and the Fairy of the Pine Woods, the Cherry Blossom Fairy, and the Fairy of the Song Birds. One gave the baby the gift of dancing, and one the gift of music. One gave her the gift of beauty, and one the gift of song.

"Just like the story," thought Anna. She wanted to whisper, "Isn't it lovely?" to her mother, but she could not turn her eyes away from the stage even for a second, for now the fairies were dancing.

The Fairy of the Pine Woods danced slowly and

gracefully to soft, sleepy music. The Cherry Blossom Fairy jumped and whirled faster and faster. The Fairy of the Song Birds gave a quick little fluttering dance, but the Lilac Fairy's dance was the best of all. Her feet moved like magic to the gay, silvery music. She jumped and spun and turned in the air. She stepped and ran, and twirled on her toes.

"How wonderful," thought Anna. "How wonderful!"

She forgot that she was a poor little girl in a shabby frock. She thought that she was the Lilac Fairy dancing up there on the stage—pointing her toes and fluttering her arms, and dancing and dancing in delight.

So the ballet went on, telling the old story that Anna knew so well, of how the princess grew up and pricked her finger, and fell asleep, and how the prince came to waken her.

Anna leaned forward, noticing every frock, and every step of the dancing—listening to every note of the music. Oh, it was wonderful! It was like a dream—a long, perfect dream. How well the princess danced! Oh, to dance like that! It seemed to Anna now, that she was the princess, rising on her toes, spreading wide her arms—jumping, whirling, dancing and dancing.

47

Suddenly the ballet was over, and the curtains closed, hanging again in long velvet folds. The lights went up, and people put on their coats and cloaks, and began chattering, and walking to the doors.

Anna's eyes were like stars, and her thoughts were still with "The Sleeping Beauty". She did not hear when her mother spoke to her, and when they went into the street, she scarcely felt the cold wind and the snowflakes that whirled in her face.

Mother held her hand tightly, and hurried her away from the theatre. This was the land of Russia, and there were horses pulling sleighs along the wide streets. The sound of muffled footsteps mingled with the music of sleigh bells over the white snow. But the music ringing in Anna's ears was the music of the ballet. She said not a word. She only held her mother's hand, and hurried along beside her.

"She must be tired," thought Mother.

Soon they reached the narrow street where they lived, and came to their own small house. Mother opened the door, and held it for Anna to go through. But Anna stood silent a moment on the dark pavement, with the cold wind tugging at her shabby coat, and the snow blowing round her.

"Mother," she said, "I know now what I am going to be when I grow up! I am going to be a dancer."

"Are you, dear?" replied Mother, and she smiled, for she knew that little girls of eight changed their minds a dozen times before they grew up.

But Anna did not change her mind. She wanted to be a dancer, and she seemed to think of nothing else at all. Day by day she danced round the table, and in and out among the chairs—standing on her toes and holding up her thin arms, jumping and whirling, twisting and turning. She knelt on the floor, and rose slowly upwards like a flower opening. She fluttered her hands and leapt into the air like a bird flying. Oh, it was lovely to dance! Even at night in her dreams she danced—light airy dances to gay, silvery music.

At first her mother tried to make her think of other things.

"Dancing is not all fun and beauty," she said. "It is hard work."

"But it makes me so happy, Mother."

"Dancers have to practise and practise the same steps over and over again."

"I don't mind how hard I have to work, and how long I have to practise, if only I can be a dancer."

Mother watched Anna sometimes as she flitted round the room. There seemed something magic about her. Her feet touched the floor so lightly. Her hands moved so gracefully. She was hardly like a real little girl. She was more like a cloud drifting across the sky, or a leaf blown in the wind. And Mother knew then that Anna would never change her mind. She would always want to be a dancer. Perhaps she was born to dance.

In Russia there was a school for ballet dancers. It took children when they were ten years old, and kept them till they were sixteen. There were always hundreds and hundreds of children who wanted to go to it, but first they had tests to pass—tests in writing and arithmetic, tests in walking and moving; and only a very few children were chosen each year.

Mother explained this to Anna, and told her that if she wanted to go to the School of Dancing, she must work hard at lessons she did not like, as well as those she did like. Then when she was ten years old, she could take the tests.

"Oh, yes!" cried Anna in delight. "I *will* work hard. I will do anything to be a dancer!"

So at ten years of age she passed into the School of

Dancing. It meant leaving her mother, for it was a boarding school, and visitors were allowed only once a fortnight. At first she felt lonely and sad and shy, and she found that what Mother had said was true. Dancing was *not* all fun and beauty. It was hard work. Besides learning ordinary school lessons, she had to do exercises, and the same steps over and over again, until she

was so tired that she could hardly stand.

But she soon began to get used to it, and she soon made friends with other children. When they asked her name, she answered, "Anna Pavlova," and to herself she thought, "One day everyone in Russia will know my name, for one day I shall be a great dancer."

She practised and practised, and when other children

went out to play or to rest, she stayed behind and practised again. Teachers and famous dancers who watched her said to each other,

"There is magic about Anna Pavlova. Surely she was born to dance!"

So the little girl Anna grew up, and all her dreams came true. She became a ballet dancer, dancing in the very theatre at which she had seen "The Sleeping Beauty" so long ago.

Everyone in Russia knew her name. She was famous. People came in crowds to watch her dance. Mother did not have to work any more. Anna bought her a beautiful house with servants; and pretty frocks and warm fur coats and shining jewels. Anna danced and danced. She was as graceful as grasses swaying in the breeze. She was as light as thistledown. She was happy because she danced.

Then one day she decided to leave Russia and dance in other countries.

"Don't go away," begged her friends. "Russians love to see ballet, but people in other countries know nothing about it. They may not like it."

"I will teach them to like it," replied Anna.

Soon the whole world was ringing with her name.

Wherever she went, people flocked to see her. They crowded into theatres and halls to watch her dance. They sent flowers to her—flowers of all kinds and colours and perfumes. They waited hours in the streets just to watch her pass.

One day as Anna left a theatre, a woman ran out from the crowd, with a baby in her arms.

"Please—I want you to touch my baby," she said. Anna smiled, and held the baby for a moment. The baby, of course, was too small to understand, but as Anna saw the joy in the mother's face, she suddenly understood how much happiness her dancing gave to people. Before this, she had danced because she loved to dance—because it made her happy. Now, she danced also because people loved to watch her—and because it made them happy.

So she went on dancing, in great theatres and tiny halls, to kings and queens, to rich and poor. She danced in England and France and Germany, in America, India, Japan. On and on through the world she danced. There was magic in her steps. She was so light, so airy, like a cloud drifting across the sky, like a leaf blown in the wind. And the world was happy when Anna Pavlova danced.

Things to Do

1. See how quickly you can write these names on paper. They must all begin with **B**:

   The name of a country, a town, a boy, a girl, a fruit, an animal, a bird.

   Now do the same again, choosing the letter yourself.

2. Pretend you have landed on an island. On it there is a small wood, a stream, a hill, a cave, a ruined cottage and four fruit trees. Draw a map of the island, any shape you like. On the map draw tiny pictures, like those above, to show where the different places and things are found. Write the name beside each one.

   Give a name to the island, and to the sea that surrounds it.

3. Where did the children work whom Lord Shaftesbury helped to set free?

4. Write the names of some of the things Don saw when he was walking about on the floor of the sea.

5. Write the names of the fairies who came with a present and a wish for the little princess.

6. Try to write a poem. If you cannot think how to start, here is something to help you.

Pretend you are asking someone to come out with you. Tell him all the interesting things you will show him. You could begin this way:

Oh, do come out and play with me. I'll take you to our ——

7. Pretend you had to stay at home one morning to look after a baby and a puppy while your mother went to town. Tell of all the things that happened.

Reynard

In the middle of Hazel Wood, in a small patch of grass, grew a great oak tree. Its twisted roots sheltered many wild creatures, and there in a deep burrow lived a mother fox and her three cubs. The babies were pretty little things, just like balls of yellow-red fluff, with sharp faces and bright eyes; and they rolled and romped like puppies.

One night when they were only a few weeks old, their mother went out hunting, and did not come back. The cubs did not know what had happened to her, and for several days they lay in the burrow, crying and calling, until they were weak with hunger. One of them, a little braver than the others, began to drag himself slowly up the tunnel towards the daylight.

Soon after, a farmer passed that way, and noticed what he thought was a little bundle of brown fur lying on the grass. How surprised he was to find that it was a little fox cub! He picked him up, and took him home. His children were delighted, and wanted to play with the little fox, but the farmer took him to the barn where his dog was lying with her puppies. He made room for the cub, and put him to feed with the others. The mother dog did not mind, and soon the cub was sleeping among his new brothers and sisters.

The next morning when the children went to look at their new pet, they could see that he was feeling better, and they talked a great deal about whose pet he should be. But their father settled it by saying that as one had some rabbits, and another had some bantam fowls, the baby fox should belong to Kitty, who, you may be sure, was delighted.

At school she had been reading a story about a fox called Reynard, so she said that this would be a good name for him.

She brought her friends to see him, and they all liked her strange pet.

Reynard grew until he was no longer a fluffy ball of fur, but a handsome fox with a long nose, bright eyes, and a bushy tail with a white tip. He loved to play games with his dog brothers and sisters, and to growl and snap as they romped together in the garden. He soon learnt to answer to his name, but only when Kitty called him.

One day Kitty decided to take him for a walk in the village. She found an old dog collar and lead, and after some trouble she managed to get the collar round

Reynard's neck. Off she went, feeling very proud with her fox trotting by her side. She met some friends in the village, and she stopped so that they could see Reynard. But Reynard did not like all these strangers, and he shrank close against her legs, trying to hide himself.

Kitty bent down to pick him up, but the lead slipped out of her hand, and Reynard was off down the road like a flash, running towards home. She called and called him, but he took no notice, and she had to run after him.

When she reached home, she found him crouching in the farthest and darkest corner of the barn. As she was alone, he was willing to come to her, but as she patted him, she could feel him trembling.

Reynard grew braver as he grew older, and as foxes are sensible animals, he soon learnt that not all strange things are dangerous. Later he could often be seen walking in the village with Kitty, quite unafraid so long as she was near.

And then one night the trouble began. A hen disappeared. Next morning there were feathers in the henhouse and outside on the ground to show what had happened. There were still more feathers and well-picked bones in the barn where Reynard slept at night.

"Oh, Reynard," Kitty cried, "how could you kill the chicken? Whatever will Daddy say?"

But Reynard looked back at her without understand-standing. He did not know what all the fuss was about. It was in his nature to hunt for food and he could not help killing fowls, though he was clever enough to sense that Kitty was angry and upset.

"What's all this?" said her father, frowning over the feathers. "Well, that decides it, Kitty. I'm sorry, but you cannot keep your pet any longer. You can't make a wild animal into a tame one. I have had complaints about missing hens from the neighbours lately, and I began to think that Reynard was the cause."

"Give him one more chance, Daddy," cried Kitty.

"No, it would not be fair to Reynard," Daddy answered. "You would have to shut him up at nights, just when he was longing to be out hunting like other foxes. He will fret and become unhappy. You cannot treat him like a dog. As it is, I shall have to be very careful of my hens."

"Then what must I do, Daddy?" Kitty asked.

"You must let him go. Take him back into the country," her father answered. "You remember the place I once showed you, where I noticed a family of cubs? Well, leave him there. He will soon meet a fox family."

Kitty obeyed with a heavy heart. She found the old dog collar once more, and in the cool of the evening she led Reynard into the country. She stopped in a place where there were thick bushes, and stooped down to take off his collar.

"I am so sorry, Reynard," she said. "I wish you could stay. I shall be lonely without you." She patted his handsome back, and then turned quickly and went home as fast as she could.

She half hoped that Reynard would follow her, or

come back to the barn at nightfall, but Reynard behaved like the fox he was. He was free. Being a wild animal, he did not even stop to watch Kitty go, as a dog would have done, but he trotted off quickly into the bushes to look for fox friends. He had learnt much about humans from living among them, and he was not at all puzzled because Kitty had left him. He soon found a family of foxes, and was quite happy.

As for Kitty, she went home through the fields, still hoping that Reynard would slip back to the farm. When she reached the house, however, her father met her. He knew she would miss her fox, so he held out a little puppy to her.

"This is for you, Kitty," he said kindly. "I thought you would like a new pet. Take care of it."

"Thank you, Daddy," she said. "Isn't he a dear little chap?" She took the warm little puppy in her arms, and she soon forgot to look for Reynard's return.

Of course Reynard never went back. Though Kitty knew he was happier in his new home, and she no longer wanted him back, she still used to look for him sometimes when she walked in the fields.

Adapted

Where Go the Boats?

Dark brown is the river,
Golden is the sand.
It flows along for ever,
With trees on either hand.

Green leaves a-floating,
Castles of the foam,
Boats of mine a-boating—
Where will all come home?

On goes the river
And out past the mill,
Away down the valley,
Away down the hill.

Away down the river,
A hundred miles or more,
Other little children
Shall bring my boats ashore.

ROBERT LOUIS STEVENSON

The Boy who Liked Music

Nanerl was learning to play the clavier. The clavier was like a piano, only smaller. She sat up straight on the stool to do her practising. Her legs dangled, and did not nearly reach the floor, for she was only eight years old. She pressed down the little white keys with her fingers, just as the music book showed her. The soft, gay little tune she played went lilting through the house. In another room her three-year-old brother Wolfgang was playing with his toys. He heard the music, and sat still for a moment, listening. Then he jumped up from the floor, and ran into the room where the clavier was.

He held out his arms to Nanerl, and she lifted him

on to her lap, and went on playing as well as she could.

"Let me try," said Wolfgang.

"All right," laughed Nanerl.

Wolfgang was only a baby, and she thought he would just bang notes anywhere, and make a jangling noise, but he didn't. He put two fingers carefully on two notes, leaving out one in between. It made quite a pleasant sound. He did it again with two more notes, leaving out one in between.

"I can make music," he said happily, and he went all the way up the clavier, and all the way down again, playing chords with his baby fingers.

After that, he took a great interest in Nanerl's music lessons, and he surprised everyone by remembering little pieces from her music book, and playing them himself.

"I want to learn music," he said. He said it so many times that his father began teaching him in fun. Wolfgang learnt very quickly, and could soon play a number of pieces perfectly. When he was four years old, he started making up his own tunes and playing them on the clavier. His mother and father were amazed.

"Wolfgang is a wonder child!" they said.

By the time Nanerl was eleven and Wolfgang was six,

they could play the clavier so well that their father decided to show his two clever children to the world. He took them to the great cities of Europe—first to Munich, and then to Vienna.

In Vienna a message came from the Empress, asking the children to go to the palace and play to her. How excited they were! Their mother dressed them in their finest clothes, and brushed their hair till it shone. Nanerl wore a white silk frock, and Wolfgang wore a suit trimmed with broad, gold braid. They arrived at the palace, where the Empress welcomed them kindly.

You might think that a little boy of six would feel shy, playing to such a grand lady in such a fine palace, but Wolfgang did not mind at all. He played the clavier for a while, and then he jumped on to the Empress's lap, flung his arms round her neck, and kissed her. She was delighted with the friendly little boy and his gentle sister.

After that, the names of Wolfgang Mozart and his sister Nanerl were heard all over Europe. Everyone wanted to see these wonderful children. Everyone wanted to hear them play.

The children travelled more and more, to Germany, Austria, France, Holland and England. They must often have been tired, and sometimes they became ill, and had to rest. Then, as soon as they were better, on they would go again, playing in halls, houses, churches, making people happy to hear them, filling the world with music. And year after year as they journeyed, little Wolfgang made up tunes, hummed them in his head, wrote them down on scraps of paper, tried them on his clavier. He made tunes when he was a little boy, when he was a big boy, when he was a man.

All this happened a long while ago, but the music of Wolfgang Mozart is known and remembered today. Claviers are almost forgotten, but wherever there are pianos, violins and orchestras, his music is played. So his tunes go on lilting through the world—sad tunes, solemn tunes, gay tunes, happy tunes—on and on for ever.

Star Patterns

The stars in the sky are arranged in certain patterns. Each pattern is not always in the same place. It may be the right way up in spring, and the wrong way up in autumn. It may be at the back of your house in summer, and at the front of your house in winter. But the pattern itself does not change, and once you know it, you will be able to find it wherever it is.

Here are three easy ones to learn. Draw them so that you remember them. Then look for them next time you are out at night when the sky is clear and the stars are shining.

Cassiopeia
Cassiopeia is easy, because it is like a large W.

69

The Plough

This is like a plough with a long curved handle.

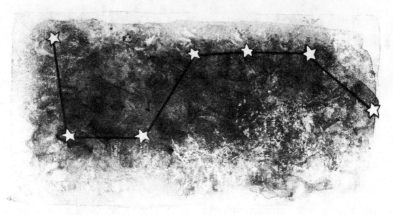

Orion

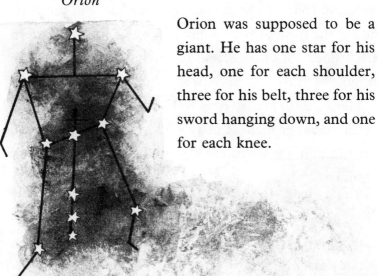

Orion was supposed to be a giant. He has one star for his head, one for each shoulder, three for his belt, three for his sword hanging down, and one for each knee.

The Jar of Olives

Once upon a time there was a man named Ali, who wished to go on a journey. As he expected to be away a long time, he sold his house and his furniture, but he could not decide what to do with his money. He had saved a thousand pieces of gold, and he wanted to leave them in a safe place until his return.

After a while, an idea came to him. He put the gold into a large jar, and then filled the upper part of the jar with olives, so that the gold was hidden. He closed the top of the jar, and then carried it to a friend of his who was a merchant.

"Will you do something for me?" he asked. "I am going away, as you know. Will you look after this jar of olives till I come back?"

"Certainly," replied the merchant. "Take it to my storeroom and put it where you like, and you will find it in the same place when you return."

Ali took the jar to the storeroom, thanked his friend for his kindness, and then started on his journey. He visited one country, and then another, travelling far and wide across the world.

At last when seven years had passed, he decided to

return to the town where he had lived before.

Now all this time, the jar of olives stood in the storehouse where he had left it. His friend the merchant scarcely thought of it at all, and for many years he even forgot about Ali. Then one night at supper, the merchant's wife began to talk of olives.

"I haven't tasted olives for a long while," she remarked.

"That reminds me," said the merchant. "There's a jar of olives in the storeroom. It belongs to Ali. What a long time he has been away! It must be seven years at

least. Surely he will never come back now. We may as well eat the olives if they are still good."

He stood up, taking a plate in one hand and a candle in the other.

"Oh, I don't think we ought to touch them," said his wife. "Ali trusted you with the jar. What will he think if he does return, and finds that you have opened it? Besides, the olives must be bad by now."

The merchant knew that his wife was right, but he would not listen to her. He went to the storeroom, and opened the jar. By the light of the candle, he saw at

once that the olives had gone bad.

"I wonder if they are *all* bad," he thought, and he tipped the jar on its side to see. As some of the olives tumbled out, there was a rattling sound, and there upon the floor fell several pieces of gold.

"Oh!" exclaimed the merchant in delight, for he was a greedy man. Then as he looked into the jar again, he found that the lower half was filled with gold, and the olives had been put in only to hide it.

Not knowing quite what to do, he put the olives back on top of the gold, covered the jar, and went back to his wife.

"You were right," he said. "The olives were bad, so I have left them as they were."

"It's a pity you touched them," she answered. "It is wrong to touch things belonging to other people."

That night the merchant hardly slept. He wanted to take Ali's gold.

"But how can I do it so that Ali will not find out even if he does return?" he said to himself. He tossed and turned and wondered and wished, and soon he thought of an idea.

Next day he went to the market and bought some olives. Then he took the gold and the old olives from the jar, and filled the jar up with the new olives. He covered the top of the jar again, and put it back where Ali had left it. The gold he took into his bedroom, where he hid it in a cupboard.

A few days later there was a knock at the door of his house. The merchant opened it, and there outside stood Ali.

"Hullo," said Ali. "I have come for my jar of olives. I hope it hasn't been in your way."

"Oh, no, it has been no trouble to me," replied the merchant. "You may take it from my storeroom. You will find it just where you left it."

So Ali carried the jar to the inn where he was staying. He opened the jar, and took out the olives from the top. There beneath them were more olives. He took those out too, expecting to see the glitter of gold beneath them. But he saw only more olives. Feeling puzzled, he tipped the jar upside down. More olives rolled out, until they were all upon the floor. There was no gold at all—not one single piece.

"This must be the wrong jar," he thought, but when he looked more carefully at it, he knew that it was not the wrong jar. For a moment he did not know what to think. Then he said aloud,

"Surely my friend, whom I trusted, has not stolen my gold from me!"

Once again he knocked at the merchant's door. The merchant was expecting this, so he had planned what to say, but he pretended to look surprised.

"What has brought you back so soon?" he asked.

"I've come about the jar of olives," replied Ali. "I know it is the same jar that I left in your storeroom, but I left a thousand pieces of gold in with the olives, and now I cannot find them."

"I have not touched your jar!" exclaimed the merchant angrily. "You left it in my care for seven years. You found it just where you had left it. Now you come and ask me for a thousand pieces of gold! I wonder you do not ask me for diamonds or pearls!"

People passing in the street heard the sound of their loud, angry voices, and drew near to listen. So very soon everyone in the town knew that Ali accused the merchant of stealing a thousand pieces of gold which were hidden in a jar of olives. Even the children began to talk about it.

Ali was unhappy because the merchant had been a bad friend to him, and he was angry because now he had no money, so he told his story to the king, and asked that the king should judge between the merchant and himself. The king agreed to do this, and commanded them both to come before him on the following day.

That evening the king dressed himself as a poor man, and wandered through the streets of the town, listening to different people talking. Nearly everyone was talking about Ali and the merchant.

"The merchant *must* have stolen the gold," said some.

"But how can it be proved?" asked others.

"That's just the trouble," thought the king to himself. "How can it be proved?"

At that moment he came upon a group of children playing at the side of the path. He stood back in the shadows and listened to their game. Strangely enough, they were playing at Ali and the merchant, and one boy was sitting on the ground pretending to be the king.

"Ali," he was saying, "let me see the jar of olives which you left with the merchant for seven years."

The child who was supposed to be Ali handed him

a jar, and the boy-king looked inside it.

"These are fine olives," he remarked, pretending to eat one. Then he stopped suddenly, and said, puzzled, "Surely olives would be bad after seven years!"

"Ah!" thought the king. "There is the proof I need."

Next day Ali and the merchant went before the king, and a crowd of people gathered round to listen. Ali told his story again, and the merchant said once more that he had not touched the olives.

"Ali," said the king, "let me see the jar of olives."

Ali handed it to the king, and the king looked inside.

"These are fine olives," said the king, tasting one. "I did not know olives could be kept for seven years, and still be good."

He turned to a messenger, and said,

"Bring me an olive merchant."

After a few moments an olive merchant was brought forward.

"Tell me," said the king. "How long will olives keep, and still be good to eat?"

The olive merchant bowed low, and replied in a grave voice,

"Not more than two years, Your Majesty. By the third year they will have no taste and no colour."

"Then," said the king, "look at these olives, and tell me how long it is since they were put into this jar."

The merchant looked, tasted the olives, and answered, "They are good olives, new this year, Your Majesty."

"But Ali says he put them in the jar seven years ago, and this merchant here says that he has not touched them in all that time," said the king.

"No, Your Majesty," said the olive merchant. "These olives have been picked this year. Anyone will tell you the same."

So it was proved that Ali's olives had been taken out of the jar, and changed for new ones. Only the merchant could have changed them, and therefore he must have taken the gold as well. He was ordered to return the thousand pieces of gold to Ali, which he did—every one.

As for the boy who had pretended to be the king in the game of the night before, he was surprised and delighted when a messenger from the palace knocked at his door, and gave him a purse with a hundred pieces of gold inside it.

"This," said the messenger, "is a present from the king—for a very clever boy."

Adapted

Deno All Alone

Deno lived in a lighthouse with her mother and father. It was made of stone, and built on a bank of small stones, with the light fixed high on the top of a steel tower. There was sea all round, but land was not far away, and whenever food and coal and oil were running low, the family would go across to the town by rowing boat to do the shopping.

Deno liked going to town, and playing and talking for a while with her friends, and perhaps taking a turn at the oars on the way home. But she liked the loneliness of the lighthouse too, with the gulls that flew by in the daytime, and the light that shone out at night. She knew how important it was that the lamp should be kept burning through the hours of darkness, flashing its warning to ships at sea.

Now Deno's birthday was in March, and every year when it drew near, there was, of course, very special shopping for her mother and father to do when they went to town.

But one year March was wild and stormy. The waves thundered up on the beach in foaming anger, and the sea-gulls screamed and cried and flew away to the land. The wind howled round the lighthouse, and the sea tossed and roared.

"We can't go ashore today," said Deno's father. "Perhaps the weather will be better tomorrow."

He said this many times, but days and days went by, and still the storm continued.

A week passed. The food in the house was beginning to get low.

"We mustn't eat so much," said Deno's mother with a smile.

"The weather is sure to change soon," said her father. "Tomorrow perhaps." But it did not change.

Eight days passed—nine days, ten days, eleven days —two weeks. Mother and Father ate less and less, so that there should be food enough for Deno. Deno's birthday came, and still the rowing boat could not cross the angry sea. So instead of a special birthday tea, with all sorts of nice things to eat, there was scarcely anything on the table at all.

Every day the family watched the sea. If the waves would quieten down just for a little while, the rowing boat could be taken across.

Then came a day when the only food left in the house

was half a loaf of bread. There was not a scrap of anything else.

"We'll *have* to go today," said Deno's father. Anxiously he watched and waited for a chance. The sea was as high as ever, but later on it sank back a little, and the wind was not quite so strong.

"Now!" he said.

He had decided that his wife should go with him to help carry the provisions to the boat, but that Deno should stay at home.

"We won't be long," said Deno's mother with a wave of her hand. The little boat was launched, and bravely it set off across the strip of sea.

When the mother and father reached the shore, they quickly collected their food, oil and coal, and hurried back to the beach with it. At any moment the gale might grow stronger again. There was no time to spare. But as they ran to the place where they had left the boat, they saw that they were too late. The wind was blowing more strongly than before, and the waves were greater and more terrible than they had been all through the month. No little boat could sail on such a sea.

There were some fishermen standing near.

"You can't possibly go back today," they said.

"But I must!" cried the lighthouse keeper. "I must light the lamp. Besides, Deno is all alone out there, and she is hungry."

"Try my motor boat," said someone, so the food was packed into that. But even the motor boat could not travel in the storm. It was tossed from one wave to another and would have been swamped and lost if it had tried to go any further.

Sadly Deno's mother and father stood on the shore again. They knew that they would be drowned if they tried to go through that sea. They gazed across at the lighthouse. They could see it, but they could not get to it. Deno was all alone out there, and she was hungry, and when darkness came, the light would not be lit. How many ships might be lost in the storm without the light to guide them?

Meanwhile Deno was curled up in a chair, reading a book. It was an interesting book, so the time passed quickly. She felt very hungry at dinner time—but never mind. Mother and Father would soon be back with plenty of food, and oh, what a feast they would have then!

Afternoon came, but Mother and Father did not come back. Deno knew they would not visit friends today. She knew they would come back as quickly as possible, before the storm grew worse. She put down her book, and looked out of the window.

The storm *had* grown worse. Oh, dear! It was worse than it had been all the past three weeks. Waves crashed on the shore with the noise of thunder. The air was filled with the mist of splashing spray. A lonely sea-gull battled against the wind, and then dropped helplessly on the stones. Even a sea-gull, with its powerful wings, could not fly in such a gale. Certainly a little boat would not be able to sail. Deno knew that Mother and Father would not possibly be able to get back that night.

"Oh, dear," she said aloud, "I'm *so* hungry." Oh, well, she could eat up the half loaf. She would have a good meal tomorrow when Mother and Father came home, and a fire to keep her warm as well. She cut a slice of bread, and while she was eating it, she started cutting another. Then she thought,

"Perhaps I'd better *not* eat it all—just in case—"

The afternoon passed slowly, and daylight began to fade. Deno had a drink of water, just for something to do.

"I'll go to bed very early, before it gets dark, and I'll lie in bed and read," she said to herself. "I'll keep warmer that way, and perhaps I'll finish my book." Then a thought came to her. It came so suddenly that she stopped, with the cup held to her lips.

"The light! What about the light? *I'll* have to keep it burning. I'd better see to it quickly before dark." She put on her thickest sweater and set out.

This was no easy lighthouse, where she would have to walk up a winding staircase, and turn on a switch. Oh, no. This was a lamp that burned oil. The glass had to be kept clean and shining. The wick had to be trimmed. The lamp had to be kept filled with oil. And to light it, she would have to climb up an iron ladder outside the tower, up and up in the wind and spray; and at the top there was a heavy iron door to open. She would have to climb through the doorway, and light the lamp. It was not an easy job. Even Father found it hard work in bad weather.

Deno was cold and hungry, and as she went out of the door of the house, the wind rushed at her with such force that she could scarcely breathe. She struggled to the ladder, held on tightly to the rails, and started to climb. The higher she climbed, the harder it became. Her jeans flapped against her legs. Spray filled her eyes, and half blinded her. The wind blew so fiercely, so wildly that she had to cling on with all her might, and all the time the waves broke on the stones with a deafening roar.

What a long way up it seemed. What a *long* way! She felt strange because she was so hungry. Her hands were *so* cold, and her lips tasted salty like the sea.

What a long way, up and up and up, through the spray and the wind. What a long way.

At last she reached the top. There was the iron door in front of her eyes. She had only to open it and climb through. At least it would be sheltered from the wind, there inside with the lamp. She turned the handle, and

pulled the door. It did not move. It was heavy—made of iron—and the wind was blowing against it. She pulled and pulled. Once it opened just a crack, and slammed shut again. Even Father had a job to open it in windy weather. So how could Deno possibly do it—all alone?

She pulled again. She pulled and pulled.

"I'll have to leave it," she said to herself at last, "I won't be able to light the lamp."

She rested a moment, clinging to the ladder far, far above the sea, and there came into her mind the thought of ships out in the storm. Soon it would be dark, quite dark. Sailors would be looking for the lighthouse beam. How would they find their way without the light to guide them? If she didn't light the lamp, ships might be wrecked tonight. She *must* light the lamp. She *must*.

The short rest had given her new strength. Once more she pulled and pulled at the iron door, and this time it opened.

Away on the shore, her mother and father were worrying about her, and worrying about the light. It would not be lit tonight, and ships would be lost in the storm. Darkness was falling now, and the lighthouse was hidden in cloud and mist. Sadly they looked across the angry water, and suddenly, as they looked, a beam of light shone out, clearly, brightly. Deno had lit the lamp, and all night long it flashed its warning to ships at sea.

*　　*　　*

Morning came, and still the storm raged. Several brave fishermen tried to get boats out to the lighthouse, but again they failed. Everyone knew that Deno must be weak with hunger, yet no one could do anything to help her. Yet when night came, the light shone out bravely across the water once more. Deno had lit the lamp for the second time.

The next day the same thing happened. The storm raged. Boats tried to reach the lighthouse and failed. Mother and Father were almost ill with worry. Deno must be starving—simply starving! Yet for a third night the lighthouse beam flashed across the sea, warning and guiding ships in the storm. For a third time, in spite of cold and hunger, and wind and spray, Deno had managed somehow to light the lamp.

Morning came once more. Still the storm raged. For three days and nights now, Deno had been all alone. Would no one ever come to help her? Would Mother and Father never get through the gale, and bring food for her and oil for the lamp? She was hungry, so hungry, and the oil for the lamp was low, so low. To Deno it all seemed like a strange lonely dream, that went on and on, day and night.

Suddenly, in the afternoon, she saw a boat. Then a mighty wave rose, and hid it from view. Perhaps it hadn't been a boat at all. Then it appeared again. It was the lifeboat, with all the lifeboat crew, and her mother and father in it!

"Oh!" whispered Deno. "At last! At last!"

Anxiously she pressed her face to the window, watching the boat battle with the waves. Oh! It couldn't land! The waves just played with it as if it were a toy. Wildly the wind blew, and the sea thundered. Up in the spray went the lifeboat, and then down in the depths of the waves. Up again and down again, up and down, up and down.

"Oh!" murmured Deno. "Will they ever do it?"

Then there was the crunching sound of wood on stones. Several of the crew were jumping waist deep,

shoulder deep, into the water. The lifeboat was landing! Mother and Father were climbing out, with food and coal and oil. Mother and Father were home again. Deno was saved.

If you ever go to the Isle of Wight for a holiday, you may see the Bembridge Lighthouse, where Deno lived. Everyone called her Deno, but her real name was Ethel Langton.

Perhaps when it is dark, you will see the light flashing out across the sea, and then you will remember how brave Deno kept it burning for three stormy nights when she was all alone.

The Story of a Road

Once upon a time, hundreds of years ago, there was a little footpath. It was rough, narrow and stony. The only people who used it were the farmer taking his cows to the meadow, and the children wandering round the side of the hill, on their way to the village. But as the years went by, the path became a little flatter where the cows' hooves wore it down, and a little wider where the children ran over the edge of it.

Not far away stood a castle where a rich man lived. He had two castles—a winter one and a summer one. It was time now to go to the summer one, so all his family and his servants began to prepare for the journey. The rich man had noticed the footpath getting wider and smoother, and he said,

"We will go that way this time. It will make our journey much shorter."

So very soon the little footpath felt the trotting of horses' feet, and the rumbling of wooden wheels. It felt proud to think that so many grand people were riding along on it.

The rich man was dressed in beautiful clothes of scarlet and blue, and the horse on which he rode had a

purple cloth on its back. Two servants rode beside him,
and seven more followed. Then came a carriage the
colour of gold, with the rich man's wife and his four
little children jogging up and down inside it.

After that came oxen pulling three slow, creaking
carts filled with luggage, and then came seven more
servants on prancing horses. The sun shone on the
cloths of blue and scarlet, and on the purple tassels
that hung from the horses' heads. It danced on the
golden carriage, dazzling the eyes of the little village

boys and girls, who stopped to stare in wonder. It was like the procession of a king!

In those days no one travelled unless they had a good reason. In the winter, roads were flooded by rain. Wagons stuck in the mud, and their wheels made great ruts and holes. People were likely to lose their way, and often there were animals and robbers about.

It was the journey of the rich man and his family that really changed the little footpath from a footpath to a road. The horses' hooves scattered the dust. The wooden wheels flattened down the grass at the sides.

Next day a pedlar, trudging along the highroad with a bag of pretty things to sell, looked across the grass, and noticed the path beyond the castle.

"Ah!" he said. "A short cut! I'll go this way."

Then a company of merchants passed along, on horseback. The horses carried bundles of cloth to be sold; and small bells jingled to warn people of their coming.

So the footpath became wide and worn, and more and more people used it. Minstrels passed that way, humming the tunes they meant to play upon their pipes at inns and castles. Jugglers and dancers went to earn some money at the village fair. Messengers carried letters.

The road was made wider still, and bushes at the side were cut down. No longer was it a little footpath that hardly anyone used. It was a busy highway.

The village became more important too, with so many people passing through it. The innkeeper had to put more beds in his inn, and his wife was kept very busy cooking meals for hungry travellers. Each day as the sun sank to rest, bells rang out from the church, and a pot of fire was hung up in the tower to guide people who still wandered in the dark.

For years and years the road wound at the side of the hill. In summer it was rough and stony and dusty. In winter parts of it were washed away by rain, or buried beneath snow. Sometimes a farmer filled up a few of the holes, or the people of the church dug a ditch at the side to drain the water away. But apart from this no one ever bothered to keep the road in good repair. Yet still the traffic went on, round the hill, and into the village.

It would take too long to tell of all the feet that walked, and all the wheels that rolled along the highway. Carts and wagons and carriages changed. People's clothes and ideas changed. And the years passed by, and the years passed by, until five hundred years had gone.

Then came a man called John McAdam. He brought workmen and tools. He straightened the road, cutting away some of the twists and turns. He built a new smooth surface to it, like a strong, solid floor, that could bear heavy weights.

By that time people travelled by stage coach, drawn by horses. The coach was gaily painted, and had the names of the places to which it went, written on the door. The driver sat high up at the front. Some passengers sat inside the coach, and others outside. The horses galloped for 16 kilometres, and were then taken to the stable of an inn, to rest. Different horses were obtained, and the coach continued its journey.

On John McAdam's roads, stage coaches could travel much faster. Wheels could whirl round swiftly. Horses could gallop like the wind. Each driver tried to go faster still, faster than any other driver in the country. People who had long journeys to make were scarcely given time to eat their dinner when the stage coach stopped at an inn.

"Ready!" the coachman would call, blowing his horn to show that he was just starting off again. Half the food would be left uneaten on the plates. The people would scramble into the coach, and the fresh horses would pull it on its way.

More and more stage coaches used the road, wheels whirring, horses galloping, faster, faster, faster.

And then one year the road saw a strange puffing coach in the distance where the rich man's castle had once been. George Stephenson was building trains. Engines were driven by steam and did not have to rest like horses. They were faster than stage coaches, or anything else on the road.

People who had to travel now travelled by train. The stage coaches disappeared altogether. Some were left to fall to pieces in stable yards. Others were used by farmers as houses for hens. No one seemed to want the road any more. Bushes grew nearer and blocked the way. Grass crept over the edges, and weeds pushed up through McAdam's fine road. The busy highway began to look like the little footpath it had been five hundred years ago.

"My days are over," thought the road. "No one needs me now."

Only the birds flew above it, and little wild rabbits chased each other across it.

For fifty years the road slept.

Then one day it was awakened by a strange sound. A man was walking along, holding a red flag. Behind him came a queer snorting thing on wheels.

"A stage coach at last," thought the road, but it was not a stage coach, for it was not pulled by horses. It just seemed to go by itself, jerking, banging, rattling. A crowd of people followed. They laughed and pointed and chattered. They had come to watch the first motor car they had ever seen.

·   ·   ·   ·   ·   ·

The road still winds round the side of the hill, and all day long a stream of traffic passes by. There are cars and bicycles, vans and lorries—hurrying, overtaking each other, speeding along the fine modern road—faster, faster, faster.

The road now has scarcely a moment in which to remember the children who stopped to stare at the first slow, golden carriage, or the minstrels, the jugglers and the dancers going to the fair, or the merchants and the messengers of six hundred years ago. Only sometimes, when the night is dark, and the late motor cars have flashed their headlamps and whizzed by, it hears again the jingling of bells, the clatter of horses' hooves, and the blowing of the stage coach horn. As it winds round the hillside, white and shining in the blackness, it dreams of days of long ago.

Travel

To travel from London to Edinburgh used to take forty days on horseback. In Queen Elizabeth I's reign someone did it in three days and two nights. Today the journey takes under eight hours by train or ten hours by car.

From a Railway Carriage

Faster than fairies, faster than witches,
Bridges and houses, hedges and ditches;
And charging along like troops in a battle
All through the meadows the horses and cattle:
All of the sights of the hill and the plain
Fly as thick as driving rain;
And ever again, in the wink of an eye,
Painted stations whistle by.

Here is a child who clambers and scrambles,
All by himself and gathering brambles;
Here is a tramp who stands and gazes;
And there is the green for stringing the daisies!
Here is a cart run away in the road
Lumping along with man and load;
And here is a mill, and there is a river:
Each a glimpse and gone for ever!

ROBERT LOUIS STEVENSON

Do You Know?

Some Spiders Have Parachutes

Have you ever noticed that some mornings when you go outside, there are long fine silky threads on the ground and even in the air? These silky threads look just like those used by spiders in spinning their webs. You wonder and perhaps say to yourself, "It seems as though a lot of broken spider's webs have been blown all over the place." What are these white threads that glisten in the morning dew, and look almost like frost on the ground and the bushes? Their real name is *gossamer*, and they are the threads spun by the tiny gossamer spider.

When the sun is shining and the air is warm, this tiny spider spins one or two threads on a twig or a branch. Then it holds tightly on to these fine threads and sends out some silvery streamers from its body. It uses these streamers as a parachute and jumps off into the air, with its silken parachute flying out behind it. On a windy morning the tiny spider, with many other friends, is blown along over the fields.

Some of the threads of these tiny fliers catch on the bushes or fall to the ground, and that is what we see glistening in the dew in the early morning.

The spiders are so light that they can float along for quite a distance, leaving little pieces of their parachutes here and there.

Zonga the Hippopotamus

The sun shone down on the warm waters of the wide Zambezi River. On the bank, monkeys chattered in the trees, and swayed on the tall, slender palms. High, feathery grasses, glossy leaves and tall bushes all tangled themselves together as they tried to get a glimpse of the blue African sky.

In a deep pool of the river, just showing above the water, were two grey-brown ears, two eyes and two nostrils. They belonged to Zonga the hippopotamus, who lay waking and sleeping, dreaming and dozing through the hot day. He could see his mother not far away, lying with other hippos, half in the water and half out of it. Although Zonga looked enormous, and weighed more than three tonnes, he was still very young. He remembered how, when he was a baby, his mother had carried him on her head, and swum with him in the shallow waters. He remembered too how he had played in the river, diving in and rolling over, and swimming after a log just for fun.

He wanted to ask his mother something, so he swam over to her, leaving a great ring of widening ripples in the river. Slowly he lifted his body halfway up the sandy shallows. The water dripped from his smooth, thick skin, and fell like raindrops all around. He puffed and snorted, and settled himself beside his mother, with his head resting on her broad back. The sun gleamed and danced on his wet, shiny body.

"How beautiful my child is!" thought his mother, looking at him proudly.

"Mother," said Zonga, blinking his pink eyes.

"Yes, little son," she replied.

"Mother, have the hippos always lived in the Zambezi River?"

"Oh, no," she answered. "Once, long ago, my relations lived far away in the south, in the Orange River, but white people came, more and more white people. They made houses and farms and streets. They shot at the wild animals. They frightened them, and drove them away. Now, where my relations once lived, there are many, many white people."

"Aren't there any of your relations left in the Orange River?" asked Zonga.

His mother shook her head.

"I wish I knew," she said.

"I will find out for you," murmured Zonga with a twitch of his ears. "I should like to see the Orange

River. One day I shall walk there."

"It is a long, long way," replied his mother, "and I do not think it can be as pleasant as the warm Zambezi."

Zonga yawned. His wide mouth looked like a great cave opening. It showed his red tongue and his large, white ivory teeth. He slid further back into the river, and let the warm water wash over him again, until only his ears, his eyes and his nostrils could be seen.

In the evening the sun dipped over the river. It turned the slender palms and the tangled forest plants to gold and pink. It kissed the waters of the wide Zambezi till they glowed as red as the sky. Then it slipped away and was gone. Only then did the hippos move. They swam downstream, and grunted and snorted, and came out of the water. Zonga was glad, because he was hungry.

As the huge creatures walked along, Zonga kept close to his mother. His short legs were strong; his thick tail hung down from his back and ended in a little lock of hair.

Darkness fell, and a million stars twinkled. The air was soft and warm. Like green lanterns shone the eyes of little creatures of the night, watching the great shadows of the passing hippos. Many kilometres walked Zonga and his mother with the hippo herd. Soon they came to a long stretch of coarse grass.

"Ah!" sighed Zonga. "Just what I need." He cut down bundles of it, with his white ivory teeth. He crunched and munched to his heart's content, and all around him the other hippos did the same. When they had eaten enough, they tramped back to the river, where they had another meal of reeds and water plants. They swam to a little island, where they lay basking in the

rising sun. Then when the world really began to awaken, and the monkeys screeched a welcome to the new day, the hippos slipped into the warm Zambezi once more. Zonga let the water lap over his body, until only his ears, his eyes, and his nostrils could be seen. A great ring of widening ripples spread around him, and there he stayed, waking and sleeping, dreaming and dozing through the hot day.

Only once he roused himself to speak.

"Mother," he said. "Tonight when the herd moves north, I shall move south."

"Why, little son?"

"I shall journey to the Orange River, to see if hippos live there still."

His mother sighed a deep sigh, that sent small waves chasing one another far down the river.

"Zonga," she said slowly. "Some creatures are content to stay where they find themselves. Others must see the world. If you want to see strange, far-away places, you must go. The Orange River is a long, long way. Be careful of crocodiles and men, but most of all, be careful of white men."

Zonga nodded his huge head.

"I will come back," he said.

That night when the hippos walked out of the water, and moved north in search of food, Zonga swam to the other bank, and started his great adventure.

He travelled south, walking by night and resting by day. He passed bushes, and spreading baobab trees with trunks so broad that they looked like several trees stuck together in one. He passed green slopes with rocks scattered over them, and crimson flowers here and there, and ant hills nearly as tall as giraffes.

At last he came to the Limpopo River. Gladly he
plunged in, and rolled over and let the water cover him.
Then he lay, half in, half out, with the sun beating
down on his thick, smooth skin. In the distance two
men paddled a rough wooden canoe. In and out dipped
their paddles, in and out, in and out. Nearer and nearer
they came. Zonga listened to the sound, and slipped
further into the water, so that only his ears, eyes and
nostrils could be seen.

"What is that strange creature coming this way?"
he said to himself. "Is it a crocodile? No—it is not a
crocodile. What can it be?"

Because he had not seen a canoe since he was very, very small, Zonga became frightened.

"I must attack it," he thought, "before it attacks me."

He dashed suddenly through the water, rushed at the canoe, and tore out the side of it with his white ivory teeth. The broken canoe tipped over and began to sink. The terrified men fell into the river, and swam for the shore. Zonga snapped at the canoe again, and crunched the crumbling wood, then let it sink to the bottom of the Limpopo.

"Ah!" he said. "I have killed it!"

He puffed and snorted, and blew a spout of water into the air.

At that moment he saw something else moving near the bank. He saw a great grey-brown body, wet and shining. It was a hippo. He saw another and another. Zonga swam to them. They spoke to him kindly.

"You are still very young," they said.

Zonga was surprised, for he was beginning to think by now that he was a grown-up hippo.

"Why do you say that?" he asked.

"Because you were so foolish as to attack a canoe, when it was not hurting you at all."

"A canoe?" he repeated in a puzzled voice. "Is that the name of the animal I killed?"

"Animal!" laughed one of the hippos. "It was no animal, but just an old wooden boat, paddled along by two men."

"Now that you have frightened them," added a very old hippo, "they will probably come back later, to hunt and kill us."

"What good would we be to them?" asked Zonga, feeling awkward and shy about the whole affair.

"They would use our flesh for meat, and our thick skin for making whips. Our ivory teeth they would sell to other men, who would carve them into bangles, and keys for making music on pianos."

"What are pianos?" asked Zonga.

"I do not know," answered the old hippo rather crossly. "I know a lot of things, because I have seen many men and heard them speak, but I do not know everything."

"Now," he added, turning to the herd, "we must swim quickly far down the river."

"Oh, I am sorry you will have to move," murmured Zonga. "I will never attack a canoe again—unless of course it attacks me."

"Never mind," said the other hippos kindly, and they dived into the deep water. They swam away

and away, leaving Zonga lying in the shallows, hot and unhappy, with little drops of red perspiration covering his face and his body.

"I'd better move too," he thought after a little while, so he swam down the Limpopo River towards the east, and then he waded out and walked towards the south.

This was pleasant country, with trees and bushes and wild animals. He stopped to speak to a giraffe, and a number of leaping deer. Then he came to a dusty road. He stood in the middle of it and looked both ways. A car came towards him.

"Oh dear," said Zonga. "Whatever is this great red creature coming along? Is it an elephant? No— it is not an elephant. What can it be?"

Because he had never seen a car before, Zonga became frightened.

"I must attack it," he thought, "before it attacks me." He was just going to rush at it, when he remembered the canoe. That had not been an animal at all, but just an old wooden boat. Perhaps this thing was not an animal either. Perhaps it was a piano. Better hide and let it pass.

Zonga stood behind a bush, and the red car snorted past. It did not even seem to look at him. How strange!

Zonga crossed the road, and walked on through the trees. He met an elephant, who spoke to him kindly.

"You are still very young," said the elephant, and again Zonga was surprised, for he was thinking that he was quite a grown-up hippo.

"Why do you say that?" he asked. The elephant swung his long trunk, and answered,

"Because you are unwise enough to walk about in the daytime. Good hippos leave the water only after sunset."

"Oh, yes!" exclaimed Zonga. "I had forgotten."

"If you walk a little farther," said the elephant, "you will come to a pool where you may rest till dark."

"Thank you," said Zonga. Then he added, "I saw a strange red thing rush snorting past on a dusty road today. Was it a piano?"

"Piano!" laughed the elephant. "It must have been a car."

"What is a car?" asked Zonga.

"It's a kind of box in which people ride," replied the elephant. "It is not an animal."

"Oh," murmured Zonga, thinking to himself, "What strange things I have seen—a canoe and a car."

He went on a little way, and soon he came to the pool the elephant had mentioned. He waded into the still water, and there he rested till the end of the day. He was warm and wet and comfortable.

So he continued his journey, travelling chiefly by night when the sky was alight with stars, and the moon sent queer shadows leaping among the bushes. He found grass and reeds and water plants to eat. He met all kinds of animals, and crossed other dusty roads. Sometimes he heard a hungry lion roar, or the long, weird laugh of a roaming hyena. He met another herd of hippos, and he told them he was looking for the Orange River.

"You must go a little to the west and a little to the south, and a little to the west and a little to the south," they said, "but it will take you many weeks. Keep away from towns, for remember, there are houses and streets where once wild animals lived."

That night Zonga went a little to the west, as the hippos had told him. He trudged steadily along in the darkness. Soon he smelled a new smell.

"Surely this is the sweetest, most beautiful smell in the whole world!" he said. "What can it be?"

Then the moon shone, and showed Zonga what it was that smelled so sweet. He was walking between rows and rows and rows of orange trees. In the moonlight he could see dark green leaves and white blos-

soms and golden oranges all growing together, filling the air with their beauty and the sweetness of their scent.

One night he stood on a hill, and saw to the west thousands and thousands of twinkling lights.

"That is strange," said Zonga. "The stars have fallen down to earth," but when he looked up at the sky, he saw that the stars were still there. He looked to the west again. What could those lights be?

"Perhaps it is an animal with a thousand eyes," he thought. "I'd better attack it before it attacks me."

Then he remembered the canoe. That had not been an animal. He remembered the car. That had not been an animal. Perhaps this was not an animal. He had better hide and wait until morning.

But when morning came, the lights went out, and the twinkling eyes disappeared, and instead he saw great buildings like fat, white trees stretching up to the sky. Zonga could not understand at all.

He found a small, stony stream. He was longing to get really wet, for a lot of horrid little insects were digging their heads into his smooth, grey-brown skin. He stretched himself out in the water, but it was so shallow that it did not nearly cover him. A friendly little Tick Bird hopped on to his back.

"I'll help you," it said, and it pecked the horrid little insects out for him.

"Tell me," said Zonga. "What is it over there that has a thousand shining eyes at night?"

"A town," replied the bird. "Streets and houses where people live."

"Oh," murmured Zonga. "What do people do? Do they lie in deep pools all day like hippos?"

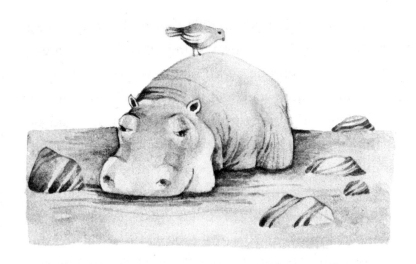

"Oh, no," said the friendly little Tick Bird. "At that town they dig deep holes in the ground and search for gold."

"What is gold?" asked Zonga, but the Tick Bird could not explain, so it flapped its wings and flew away.

It would take too long to tell of all Zonga's adventures. He saw so many new things that he couldn't even remember them all. He saw strange trees and prickly pears, and great stretches of land where there were no bushes or trees at all. He saw sheep farms, and villages where some people lived, and huts of mud and sticks where other people lived.

For weeks and weeks he journeyed—west and

south, west and south, walking by night, and resting by day. He could not always find enough grass to eat, though sometimes he tasted nice new things, like corn and maize. Often he could not find pools to swim in, and when he came to rivers, they sometimes had no water in them. He became thin and dusty and lonesome, and oh, so tired, so very, very tired. Then at last, one evening, he came to the Orange River. He knew at once that it was the Orange River. Joyfully he plunged into it, and let the cool water wash over his weary body. He dived and rolled and swam. The setting sun gleamed on the waters, turning them to pink and gold. It shone on the bare, brown hills, and the dry earth, so that they glowed in its light.

Oh, the Orange River was wide and wet, but it was not half as nice as the warm Zambezi. The bare, brown hills were beautiful in the sunset, but not half as beautiful as the swaying palms and the tangled bushes near the warm Zambezi.

"If there are any hippos here," murmured Zonga, "I will tell them to come back with me. If my mother's relations are here, I will show them the way to our home." He swam far up the river and back again, but he met no hippos.

When the moon hung low in the dark sky, he splashed up on to the bank, leaving a widening ring of ripples in the river. The water dripped from his smooth, thick skin, and fell like raindrops all around. He puffed and snorted, and the moonbeams gleamed and danced on his wet, shiny body. He opened his mouth, so that it looked like a great, dark cave. It showed his red tongue and his large white ivory teeth. He gave a loud roar—a loud, terrifying roar, the loudest, most terrifying roar that had been heard on the Orange River for nearly a hundred years.

"Are there any hippos in the Orange River? Are there any of my mother's relations here?"

Away in the distance a watch dog heard him, and barked. A little girl in bed, on a sheep farm, heard him and began to cry. A little boy, lying awake on the floor of a mud hut, heard him and trembled. But still no one answered.

Only the moon, shining down from the dark sky, seemed to whisper,

"There are no hippos here."

Only the wind, blowing through a tuft of reeds, seemed to whisper,

"There are no hippos here."

Only the Orange River itself seemed to whisper,

"There are no hippos here."

Zonga closed his huge mouth, and turned his nose towards home.

★   ★   ★

The sun shone down on the warm waters of the wide Zambezi. On the bank, monkeys chattered in the trees, and swayed in the tall, slender palms. High, feathery grasses, glossy leaves and tall bushes all tangled themselves together as they tried to get a glimpse of the blue, African sky.

Lying half in the water and half out of it was a herd of hippos. They talked of Zonga.

"It is a long time since he left," said one.

"Perhaps he cannot find the Orange River," remarked another.

"I wish he would come back," sighed Zonga's mother, and her sigh sent little waves chasing each other all the way down the river.

"Who is that swimming towards us?" asked one of the hippos suddenly. They all looked over to the deep water. There just showing above it, were two grey-brown ears, two eyes and two nostrils. It was Zonga! He had come back home, to the warm Zambezi River.

More Things to Do

1. This is a garden. Write something about it, telling what it is like. Begin like this:

    One day I went to a beautiful garden. *and*

2. Look at an atlas and find the map of Africa. Look for the Zambezi River and the Orange River. Then you will see how far Zonga walked. If you cannot find the rivers, ask someone to show you where they are.

Do You Know

How High a Hare Can Jump?

Perhaps you have seen a hare bounding away across the fields, and perhaps you have thought that he is very much like his cousin the rabbit. He is in some ways, but the rabbit is born with closed eyes and no fur, and the hare is born with his eyes open, and some fur on his body.

The rabbit spends most of his early life down in a burrow in the earth, but the young hare, or leveret as he is called, lives in a shallow hollow in the open ground.

The mother hare puts each leveret in a separate place and visits them each in turn. As the young hare grows a little older, he looks rather handsome in his reddish-brown coat, and he soon becomes very good at jumping. He can jump over quite large things, and has even been known to jump right over a small motor car.

Have you ever noticed that the front legs of a hare are much shorter than the back legs? So although he can run very quickly uphill, he has to run downhill in a zigzag fashion, to prevent himself from overbalancing.

As well as being a swift runner and a high jumper, he is also a good swimmer. He can cross a pool or a river, or even swim in the sea.

Where the Eyes of a Flatfish Are?

The eyes of a flatfish (such as a flounder or a plaice) are both on the upper side of the body. This is because these fish spend much of their time lying flat on the bed of the sea. But their eyes have not always been in that position.

When a flatfish is born, it looks like an ordinary fish, and has one eye on each side of its body in the usual way. When it is about a month old, it turns over and starts swimming on one side, and becomes much flatter. Then the eye from one side gradually moves over until it is close to the eye on the other side, and there it stays.

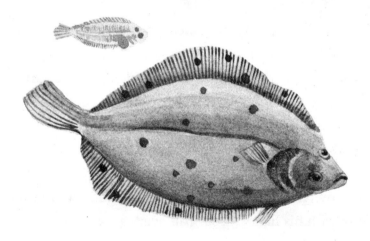

The Story of Ships

There have been waters since the world began—fast flowing rivers, still, calm lakes, and wide tossing seas. And as long as there have been people upon the earth, men have wondered where the rivers flowed, what was across the lakes, and whether there were other lands over the seas. So it was that boats were made.

The first boat was nothing but a floating log, with a cave boy lying face downwards on it, paddling himself along with his hands. Logs roll over easily, and the boy must have fallen in the water many times before he found that it was easier to manage a tree trunk which was hollowed out from one side. So his next boat was a dug-out canoe. He made it by burning out or cutting away the inside of a tree trunk, using his simple flint tools to smooth and shape it, and taking pieces of flat wood for paddles.

At about the same time someone made a raft, by binding several logs together. This kept afloat very well, but was more difficult to guide.

No one knows exactly what the first sail was like. Perhaps a small, hot boy, floating on his father's raft in the sunshine, took off the animal skin he wore, and held it up in his arms. The wind caught it and tried to blow it away. It was a game to the boy, and he held on tightly as the skin flapped in his hands. His father noticed that the raft was moving much faster than usual. He looked round, and saw that the force of the wind against his son's animal skin was sending the raft along.

It seemed a good idea. That day he made a mast from a tall, slim tree, and he fixed up a sail of skin.

People in different parts of the world had different ideas about making boats.

They tried floating on large bundles of reeds.

They made boats, kept up by bags of straw or sheep-skins filled with air.

They used boats that had logs at the side to balance them. These were hollowed-out tree trunks with two long poles fixed across them, and joined to floating logs at the sides.

They made coracles, round in shape, woven of wicker like baskets, and covered with skin.

From these small and strange beginnings of long ago grew the great sailing ships of later days—ships with square, painted sails, and oarsmen ready to row when the wind failed—ships with wooden models of men, women, lions, dragons or birds carved on the prow—ships with eyes painted on the front to help them to "see".

A single square sail hanging across the ship could of course be used only when the wind blew from the back, but gradually other sails came into use. First a small extra one was added at the front, and later sails were rigged up lengthways of the ship, fore and aft, to catch the wind whichever way it was blowing.

Sailing ships became better and better as the years went by, till they reached the height of their glory in

the ships known as clippers and windjammers. What a
wonderful sight it must have been when one of these
sped over the sea, with the wind billowing out its great,
white sails, and the sun gleaming on the blue water.
People thought that no ship of the future could ever
look more lovely, or sail more swiftly. But sailing
ships, however well made, could not travel in calm
weather, and there were many days when no wind blew.

Paddles fixed on water wheels were tried next, and then came steam. Several ships were fitted with steam engines, but were used only on lakes and rivers. Many people laughed at them, and said they would never be made to work properly. Others were terrified of the noise, and the smoke and the sparks blowing out of the funnels. After a while bigger steamships were made, and tested on sea voyages, but they usually had sails as well, in case the engines failed.

Until then ships had been made of wood. Any piece of wood thrown upon water will at once float. Iron, of course, sinks. Yet shipbuilders learned the secret of shaping iron in such a way that it would float. So ships of iron were built to take the place of ships of wood.

Steamships needed to carry a great deal of coal for the engines, and the coal took up large spaces that might have been used for cargo. But they could go very

much faster than any ship of the past, and year by year they were made bigger, more comfortable, and faster still.

Then once more a new kind of ship appeared, a ship that needed no coal at all—the motor ship. Motor ships are driven by oil. Oil takes less space than coal, and ships are able to carry enough to last for long voyages.

Today there are ocean liners that are like small towns. They have shops and swimming pools on board, and rooms and cabins for thousands of people. Today too, there are aircraft carriers, and ships that take trains across the Channel. There are racing boats and warships, tankers and whalers, lifeboats and submarines. On every sea, day and night, there are ships. In every harbour, lights flash and flags fly, and some sailor gazes at new land for the first time.

The cave boy who floated down the river on a log started one of the longest stories in the world, the Story of Ships. But he did not know the end of the story.

Neither do we.